D0449351

Global Awakening
{ Core Message Series }

It is our desire to bring the messages of the Kingdom to the people of God. We have taken what we consider to be core messages from Randy Clark's sermons and schools and printed some of them in booklet form. We hope this teaching increases your understanding of God's purposes for the times we are in and that you find yourself encouraged in your faith. Other core messages are available and they are listed at the end of this booklet.

For more information on how to order this book or any of the other materials that Global Awakening offers, please contact:

Global Awakening
1451 Clark Street
Mechanicsburg, PA 17055
1-866-AWAKENING
www.globalawakening.com

{ Open Heaven }
_____
{ Are You Thirsty? }

RANDY CLARK

Table of Contents

{ Open Heaven }

I do not believe that I could have received this message had I not left the country. A lot of what I am writing about grew out of my experiences in Brazil. It grew out of an encounter or discussion in Birmingham, England, and then as these experiences came, I was able to see what was in the Bible all along but just hadn't registered. It didn't make sense. It didn't have power; it was just words. But out of what occurred, I found that the experience was scriptural and began to see things I hadn't seen before. In this teaching on the Open Heaven, I will be mentioning quite a bit about angels, but the teaching is not about angels. It is about all that has been purchased for us by the cross of Jesus Christ and what He died to make available for us. It is a fuller understanding of all that the cross merited and how it opened up heaven. We will be looking at Genesis 28 and the dream of Jacob, which I believe is one of the most profound prophetic dreams recorded in the Bible. It was both looking to and fulfilled in the new covenant in the cross of Jesus Christ.

Dealing with Old Wineskins

When I first began hearing about some of the experiences I am writing about, I didn't accept it. It was too weird, and I didn't know what to do with it; so, I just put it on the back burner, so to speak, and didn't even want to deal with it. It began for me in 1995 when I was in Birmingham, England, and I had the opportunity to meet with one of the men who had been a hero of mine. I had read about his life and had wanted to meet him since eleven years earlier (1984) when I had read John Wimber's book on signs, wonders and church growth. I had read about this man, I had heard about his stories and I said, "God, I would love to meet Omar Cabrera, the famous pioneer evangelist in Argentina." I had my opportunity. We were in this little private hotel and he and I began talking. I asked him this question, "Omar, you are a famous evangelist, and I am just getting started and don't know what I am doing. I have just been caught up in this thing and need wisdom. Is there anything you can teach me that would help me where I could see more happening in my meetings?" He looked and he said, "Yes". I said, "What?" He said, "Randy, I have never understood why you North Americans who understand the Holy Spirit, you understand the gifts of the spirit, you ask for the Holy Spirit to come and you want to move in the gifts of the spirit, but why don't you pray for God to send his angels to your meetings." Now, I have seven years of theological training. My major and minor and all my electives in college were in religion. Then, I went to seminary because by the time I graduated from that liberal college, I didn't believe enough to stay in the ministry. While in seminary I tried to play the Devil's advocate hoping that the conservative professors I had chosen would destroy those liberal arguments that I had learned in college. The difficult thing was there weren't very many conservative professors to ask. But, because of my theological training and understanding of the attributes of God, there are the big O's - omnipotence, omniscience, and omnipresence, if He is omnipotent, He has all power; if He is omniscient, He knows all things; and if He is omnipresent,

He is everywhere at once. If you have a God like that, why do you need help? I mean, if you have a God like that why would you need an angel? I have read from church history that if one gets to talking about angels, that is where it can get weird and off balance really easily. Therefore, I was a little reticent to even consider the subject. I just didn't have any place in my evangelical theology for asking God for angels. I just didn't have any room for angels. To me that was kind of a superfluous thing. It was something peripheral, that wasn't central and core to the gospel and it took away from intimacy with God. I didn't want any intermediaries between God and me. I had lots of things that just kind of rose up in my mind about why I didn't even want to think about that. So, I didn't. And so that part of the discussion was put on the back burner.

Lessons from History

When I was in New Zealand, a church elder gave me a little book. There were three books written by Owen Jorgensen about William Branham called: The Life of the Supernatural. If you do not own these books, you ought to. If you need to go sell your car, take out a line of equity in your home, or whatever you need to do to purchase those books, do so. Only the first three were completed when I started to read them. Because I have read a lot about church history, I knew that Branham ended up at the end of his life in deception, but that doesn't mean the great miracles that took place in the early part of his life were invalid. As I read these books, I literally wept. I actually wouldn't even put one down while I was getting my hair cut. I said, "This is unbelievable." I learned more about a man who was trying to learn how to cooperate with God from that material than from any other book that I had read. This was happening and I didn't understand it or know how to cooperate with it. I didn't know what to do if I had a vision. What do you do with it? As I watched him learn and make mistakes, I learned a lot. Also, it was great reading. It's a great story. My heart broke several times as I saw the brokenness of this man in his struggles with God. At that time if anyone had experienced anything like this, pastors would tell you it was the Devil instead of God. I also noticed that the angelic played a big role in his greatest miracles. So, there's another sign post. By the way, I could hardly wait until the rest of the series was finished. There are five books available now. I am sure the next one, which is going to be the last part of his life, will be off the wall when he gets into heresy. But it is written from a supportive kind of Branhamite. As my friend Bill Johnson suggests, we want to read it so we can learn how he became deceived. Hopefully, the next book in the series will give us some insight. After reading the Branham books, I started reading the Bible and suddenly, because I was thinking about this, I was seeing things that previously I had been overlooking. My problem was this: If I have the Holy Spirit, why do I need angels? Have you ever thought about that? If you have the Holy Spirit, why do you even need any angelic intervention? In my Bible reading I reached some familiar portions about Jesus' life. After he was baptized in the Jordan River and received the Holy Spirit, he was led by the Spirit into the wilderness where he was tempted by the Devil. After that time the Father sent angels to strengthen him. Who? Jesus! Here's a man who was the eternal Son of God become flesh, full of the Holy Spirit, born of the Spirit, and conceived of the Spirit. If there was anyone who was perfectly living by the Spirit, it was Jesus, the Son of God. Yet the Bible says Jesus was strengthened by angels. Now that got my curiosity up! In the Garden of Gethsemane after Jesus prayed that great prayer of agony, once again the Bible says an angel came and strengthened him. I began to think, there is something wrong here. If even the Son of God had angels come and help him, wouldn't I also need angels to come and help me? Who do I think I am? Then, I read in the Bible that an angel came and let Peter out of jail. As I continued reading the Bible, I saw that Philip was preaching a great revival and was lead by both the Spirit and angelic activity to go down to Gaza. Then, John received a revelation and didn't know how to understand all he is seeing. So God arranged for an angel to help John interpret what he was seeing in the revelation. I then read where the Apostle Paul was in a ship that was about to go down and an angel came to strengthen and encourage him. The angel told Paul what to do so that no lives would be lost. I said to myself, "Jesus, Paul, Peter, Philip and John were all in the Bible and visited by angels. The New Testament is basically full of cooperation between the Holy Spirit and angelic beings. Why have I have been so blind and resistant to this when it is so obviously present in the Bible. I then began to be more open to this thinking.

Then, I remembered that in January 1994, during the first few weeks of the outpouring in the Toronto revival, a young girl named Heather, 14 years old, came to me for prayer. She was severely dyslexic and reading at the second grade level in the eighth grade. I prayed for her and she was out under the Spirit for about 45 minutes or longer. During this time she had a vision. When the girl came to, she said she had seen herself being operated on by an angel who rewired her head. Her mother and father were pastors in the Vineyard in Hopkinsville, Kentucky, and their career before pastoring was as mental health professionals. She asked her mother to get her a book. Previously, she could hardly do math at all and it was very hard for her to read. She then began to read the book so easily. It clicked. Something had been rewired in her head. Some years later she was at a Healing School and gave her testimony. She graduated fifth in her high school class. She was also healed of allergies and some other things. Heather's best friend, Monica, was also dyslexic. When Heather returned home from being healed, she went up to Monica and said: "Monica, Jesus is going to heal you". She did not tell Monica about her healing, she just prayed for her friend. Sometime later, Monica said, "I had a vision. I saw an angel come and rewire my head". Monica was also healed of dyslexia. Later, the girls realized that both had the same vision. Suddenly I was realizing that there was more here than what I originally thought.

It is fairly well known among some of our readers that I come from a Baptist background and sometimes God uses things from my Baptist training to get a point across. You know, God has to deal with what He's got in you. He has to use your building block material to get messages to you. If you have a Methodist background, He will probably give you some Methodist stories. If you have a Baptist background, He'll give you some Baptist stories. Anyway, what he did was remind me of two things. When I was in Seminary, one of my favorite professors, Dr. Wayne Ward, was one of the few conservative men at the Seminary at that time. His teaching fellow, who was the one who did all the grading for the professor, gave a lecture one day and told this true story from his own life. This was really bizarre because at that time the Southern Baptist Seminary was very liberal theologically. This young men said, I was in Uganda and captured by soldiers that had heard there were white mercenaries in this region. I was captured along with a group of mercenaries. I could not clear up the confusion that I was a missionary not a mercenary. So, we were all to be shot in the morning. I could not convince them that I was not part of the mercenary group. They were going to kill me in the morning. I had a pocket New Testament and thought I might as well lead them all to the Lord. So I shared the gospel with the mercenaries and many of them accepted the Lord. I just knew I was going to be killed in the morning. Then somebody came into the jail where I was being held and told me that at a certain time the door is going to open and you should go out and go down around the corner where you will find a canoe. Get in the canoe and go across the lake and there will be somebody there to get you out. I never saw that person before and never saw him afterwards. Then at a certain time around 2 o'clock in the morning, it happened just like the guy said. I got away. My parents were missionaries in Africa and later I was with them. They asked me if I recalled what I was doing on a specific night, and gave the date when I was supposed to have been killed the next morning. I said, "Yes Mom and Dad, I remember where I was on that night. Why do you ask?" My Mother said, "Your father and I were awakened from our sleep by the Holy Spirit, knew you were in trouble and prayed under a great burden until the burden lifted. We were always curious as to what was going on in your life. Could you tell us?" I then told them. "I was delivered from that prison by an angel of the Lord and no one can convince me otherwise."

The other illustration from my Baptist background, that I remember, was about one of the first Protestant missionaries of the modern missionary era, excluding the Moravians: He was a Baptist named William Carey, a shoe cobbler. He got up in this big Baptist meeting in front of the leaders and said, "I feel like God is calling me to go preach the gospel to the heathen in India." Then, one of the most scholarly, well trained theological pastors of the Baptists stood up and said, "Young man, sit down, God does not need you to reach the heathen of India. God is sovereign. God can do anything he wants." Of course, both of those men were right. God can do anything He wants, but you see there is a big difference between the philosophical possibilities that God can do and the ways God has chosen. William Carey was right also. He was being called of God to go to India and preach the gospel to the heathen. All of a sudden, it dawned on me that my problem with angels was that God doesn't need them. He can do anything He wants. That was the theologian's problem with William Carey and with missionaries. He was saying God doesn't need you; He is sovereign and can do anything he wants. That's the issue. God wanted to create angels. He didn't need them; He just wanted to create them. God wanted to create human beings. He didn't need us; He just wanted to do it. It's the same thing. Humans are the army and angels are the air force and we both need to bring our acts together. That's what we are going to consider.

More Prophetic Insight

There is one other thing about how this was opened to me. In 1994, I was in Charlotte, North Carolina praying for about 400 pastors and wives. Mahesh and Bonnie Chavda were there. As I was praying, most were falling down—some were trembling, some were weeping, some were laughing, and some were crying. Bonnie motioned for me from where she was on the floor and said, "Do you want me to tell you what I am seeing?" I knew that Mahesh was a New Testament evangelist with a healing gift and Bonnie was quite prophetic. I have always been intrigued with those whom I believe to be genuine prophetic-type people. I said to Bonnie, "Yes, what do you see?" She said:

"When you started praying, instantly hundreds

of angels came into this room and started going around touching the people. The angels had pouches on and when you would go up and start praying for somebody, the angel would come right up beside you, reach in his pouch and there was like this anointing strength the angel would put into the spirit of the man or woman to strengthen them. After a while, three big angels came in that were about three feet taller than the others. The first angels were about your size, but these guys were about three feet taller and had a greater, brighter glow about them because they had been closer to the throne. They didn't have pouches and they weren't strengthening. You see they had come with a different assignment and different purpose. They had a scroll and a stamp. When you would begin to pray for somebody a big angel would come along beside you and open up the scroll that had been given to him in heaven about that person's life. As I watched him, that angel was declaring into the heavens, into the spirit realm, God's destiny over this person. Then after the angel made the declaration, he would pull out this stamp and stamp this person on the forehead."

Now I think (this is an opinion, not theology) that sometimes this gift of prophecy is worth hearing and we should begin to declare and come in agreement with what is being declared by the angel of the Lord from heaven's throne. It is found in the book of Revelation that those who didn't receive the mark of the antichrist were stamped by an angel with the mark of Christ.

Angels: On Purpose

All of this had happened in my life before I really got this message. Then the rest of the message really came alive and became more than just theology a little later on in Brazil. It was only after this experience that I got the courage to share this message. God often illustrates a teaching point with real-life experiences to help us better absorb what He wants us to learn.

We will begin at Genesis 28: 10 through 12, which says:

> 10 Jacob left Beersheba and set out for Haran. 11 When he reached a certain place, he stopped for the night because the sun had set. Taking one of the stones there, he put it under his head and lay down to sleep. 12 He had a dream in which he saw a stairway resting on the earth, with its top reaching to heaven, and the angels of God were ascending and descending on it.

Say that to yourself, "Ascending and descending on it." On what? The ladder, if you're using King James, the stairway if you're using the NIV, and if Portuguese, it is escala, where we get the word escalator. [By the way, I thought of a new name for the church but nobody thinks I'm serious. Maybe it's too far out to do but this is the name I thought about for my church: The Stairway to Heaven. Of course, I would like to take a song by Led Zeppelin, change the words to it and keep the tune, but that may be a little bit edgy for some people because there is an interest in the subject: The Stairway to Heaven.] The angels were ascending and descending on the ladder, which reached from the earth into heaven. Say it one more time—"ascending and descending on it."

> 13There above it stood the lord and he said: "I am the Lord, the God of your father Abraham and the God of Isaac. I will give you and your descendants the land on which you are lying. 14Your descendants will be like the dust of the earth, and you will spread out to the west and to the east, to the north and to the south. All peoples on earth will be blessed through you and your offspring. 15I am with you and will watch over you wherever you go, and I will bring you back to this land. I will not leave you until I have done what I have promised you." 16When Jacob awoke from his sleep, he thought, "Surely the Lord is in this place and I was not aware of it." 17He was afraid and said, "How awesome is this place! This is none other than the house of God; this is the gate of heaven."

I have told you before that I grew up in a very prejudiced era when things weren't as good as they are now, ecumenically speaking. I grew up reading J.R. Graves, that famous landmark scholar of the Southern Baptist Convention who traced Southern Baptist history all the way back through every heretical group there ever was to John the Baptist. Now I say that with tongue in cheek because if you go back and look at those groups, many of them had really, really weird views and were actually heretical in many of their views, but yet the thing was they weren't part of the Catholic Church. The doctrine was: Baptists aren't really Protestant because we never were part of the Protestant movement. We can trace our history all the way back to John the Baptist. We were looking for authority. When you don't have much to stand on, you just get louder. It was a time when we said, "Now you know the Methodists are not really churches. The Methodists are a religious society because they don't have their doctrine right. So, the Methodists are not really churches, they just have religious societies." Of course, there were lots of things said in that era about the Catholic Church too. Of course, they were also saying terrible things about us. At least we weren't burning and killing each other at that time. At least it was somewhat better than it had been.

I've had opportunities to preach in a former Church of Christ. When I was a kid growing up, the Church of Christ guy from my little town would say on radio: "I want you to know that we are the real church. You will not find the word Baptist Church, you will not find the word Methodist Church, and you will not find the word Nazarene Church. In the Bible if you really want to be biblical and want to be in a real church, there is only one name and it is the Church of Christ. I would like to just make a suggestion. Maybe more important than whether we have our polity down right, our mode of baptism down, our view of apostolic succession down, our view of instruments and non-instruments right or wrong, and maybe more than some of these doctrinal, political, governmental things, why don't we just say that a New Testament church should be like the gateway to heaven. It should be the place where there is such a presence and awareness of God that some people become afraid because the beginning of wisdom is the fear of the Lord. Why could it not be that it is the House of God where there is an experience of the Spirit so real that people realize God is in that place, even though, like Jacob they weren't aware of it. Why can't it be that way? Where we can focus more on whether or not we are pleasing to His presence rather than on those other things. Isn't it possible that we have made the commandments of God of no effect at times by imposing the traditions of man. In the new church I am starting, I'm sure there will be some things that, when we get to heaven, God is going to clarify for me and say, "You missed it on that one." But you know, I don't care, because God knows my heart and that I am trying to follow Him. I just want to love Him. But, I want my church to be a place where you can experience God regardless of where you come from. My last church in St. Louis was half former Roman Catholics. The first two missionaries we sent out were Greek Orthodox. We had Southern Baptists, Missouri Synod Lutherans, and New Age guys that grew up in bars. One of my worship leaders was a New Age guy we got out of the bar and the other guy was Roman Catholic. What brought us together was the presence of Jesus. If we were invited to minister in a Roman Catholic Church, we thanked God for it. If we were invited to preach in a Methodist Church, we thanked God for it. If we were invited to preach in a Baptist Church, we thanked God for it. I didn't want us to be a place where we find our unity only if we believe the same thing. I wanted us to find our unity because we know the same One. I started my church in the basement of a Southern Baptist home. So, we were in the basement of this Southern Baptist home and God had brought to us people who had dropped out of church and who weren't really going anywhere, but were from many different traditions. Some were just looking for a place where they could experience the presence of God a little more in their life.

The Lesson in the Lord's Supper

Let me give you an example of the unity we experienced together. The Pentecostals and Baptists have the lowest view of communion in the sense that the elements are only symbols by which you remember Jesus. They are just crackers and grape juice and nothing more before and after the prayer of consecration. Presbyterians believe that when you come in faith to receive the Lord's Supper, you are to expect to experience the real presence of Jesus. The Lutheran priest/pastor prays the prayer of consecration, and believes the body and blood of Jesus is with the elements around the literal body and blood of Jesus. The Roman Catholics, Greek Orthodox, any other kind of Orthodox, Anglicans or Episcopalians believe that when the priest prays, the outer actions which we see do not change but the inner substance becomes the literal body and blood of Jesus. So, we were taking communion in a Baptist home. After it was over, the Baptist ladies went and gathered leftovers from the Lord's Supper and headed toward the trash can, because for the Baptists or Pentecostals, they were just symbols. It had nothing to do with the body and blood of Jesus and they were getting ready to throw it away. But, on the way they passed Nicholas—by his name you would gather he is Orthodox. He said, "What are you doing?" I heard this and I thought "teachable moment". So, I taught them what I just taught you. I then said to the Baptist ladies, "Do you believe God brought Nicholas into our fellowship" and they said: "Yes, we love Nick. He is such a dear brother". I then said, "Nick do you think God brought Shirley and Helen into our fellowship?" Nick said, "Yes, I love them". I said, "Shirley and Helen, I am not asking you to believe what Nicholas believes" and "Nicholas I am not asking you to change what you believe to what they believe but if you believe God has brought us all together in one fellowship, how do we walk this out in a way that honors these differences among us and walk together in brotherly love?" The Baptist ladies said, "Nicholas, what do you do in the Orthodox Church with what's left over?" He said, "We consume it." So, for years, those Baptist ladies made sure that not one drop, from the Baptist position, of the grape juice and from the Orthodox position, the blood was thrown away. Not one crumb of the bread was ever thrown away. We consumed it. When we finally got into our building as we were growing, we had more leftovers than we used to and the ladies said, "Nicholas, this is getting kind of hard to have to eat and drink all this. Why don't we find out what the Catholics do?" So we all went to Bob, the worship leader. His mother never did learn to speak English and sang for the Pope in the Sistine Chapel—she's Italian from Italy; his wife is German Catholic, and he is Italian Catholic. We said, "Bob, what do you do in the Catholic Church?" Bob said: "We keep it and we use it again. We don't throw it away." They have a tabernacle where they put it. I said: "What do you think of that? What do you think Nicholas?" It was decided that would work and so that became our practice. Why? Because it is important to me that we be in a place where people can know we are brothers and sisters. The world will know you are my disciples by the way you love one another. Jesus said that if you can only love those who are like you, how are you any different from the world? I wanted to have this grand experiment that what brought us together was His Presence.

By the way, I think the Catholic view is the most literal of all views from Scripture, including the Baptist and Pentecostal views. I also think there is more power in the Lord's Supper, the Eucharist, than we ever thought. Paul said: "It is because you have not discerned the body that some of you have grown sick." He is saying that there is great importance to understanding the full impact of Jesus sacrificing his body for us. When Jesus gave his body, it was his body that received the stripes. It was his body from which healing came. It was his blood that purchased redemption. It was his blood that purchased forgiveness of sins and atonement.

The death of Jesus represented in the Lord's Supper is both for body and spirit; forgiveness of sins and healing of the body. When we talk about the cup, we are reminded of the purchase of forgiveness. When we talk about the bread, we are reminded of this body which was given for you. I don't like to use the word broken because I don't think it is the clear understanding of the Greek. His body was not broken as far one bone because of the Passover lamb; he said be careful not to break one bone. When they came to break Jesus legs, they did not break them because he had already given up his spirit. Now I think there were periods in the history of the church when masses of people could not read or write. I have thought a lot about communion and being in communion with him. The Greek word Eucharist basically has the root of Thanksgiving, for what he has done for us.

In a Protestant church, it's as if the gospel comes by radio. Let me explain. In a Protestant church the gospel is communicated primarily through preaching which you hear. In a Catholic church and other churches of sacramental nature, the most important thing is the celebration of the Lord's Supper, the Eucharist, the sacrifice of the mass, or whatever term you use. It's more like the gospel on television; it is not radio focused. It is television focused. Regardless of where you are, it is keeping Christ and his death in the forefront as the important thing that happens. Therefore when I went to start my last church, I wanted to make sure we shared communion every week. I can't prove to you from the Bible that you should take communion every week, but I can go to church history and tell you that the disciples of John the Apostle, the disciples of Paul and the disciples of the disciples from that point on began to have communion on a weekly basis. When I have it in my church, we will consecrate the elements of the Lord's Supper, after the first song. In my last church, we had Baptists and all these other traditions represented and I said: "Guys, you cannot consecrate it the way you did as a Baptist. Don't try to explain it, don't add stuff, just repeat His words and leave it as mystery." So after the first song and after we welcomed people, we began our service with consecration of the Lord's Supper. I would say: "On the night our Lord was betrayed He took the bread, blessed it and gave it to His disciples and said: 'This is My body which is given for you.' Likewise after the supper, He took the cup, blessed it and gave it to His disciples and said: 'This cup is the new covenant in My blood which was shed for many for the remission of sins.' Paul said: 'For as often as we eat of this bread and drink of this cup, we proclaim the Lord's death until he comes.' I then say to the people, "You may be here this morning and not be where you ought to be with God. I point you to the table of the Lord, which is a table of grace. If you have unconfessed sin in your life this morning or if you are not where you ought to be and have grown cold and indifferent, then, like John Wesley, we invite you to come, repent first and then take communion. Do not let your sin keep you from the table of the Lord. Because in communion the grace that comes to us is more than just undeserved forgiveness, it is a grace of empowering Presence to enable us to walk in holiness. So I ask you to examine yourself. To take it in an unworthy manner does not mean you have to be perfect, it means you need to come forsaking your self-righteousness and your sin and receive in grace." When we started doing that, big police officers would weep. Then we were located in a school with old tables but people would come during worship.

Open Heaven Realities

The angels of God were ascending and descending on it. The subject is the Open Heaven. I will be referring now to John 1: 47 through 51.

> 47When Jesus saw Nathanael approaching, he said of him, "Here is a true Israelite, in whom there is nothing false." 48"How do you know me?" Nathanael asked. Jesus answered, "I saw you while you were still under the fig tree before Philip called you." 49Then Nathanael declared, "Rabbi, you are the Son of God; you are the King of Israel." 50Jesus said, "You believe because I told you I saw you under the fig tree. You shall see greater things than that." 51He then added, "I tell you the truth, you shall see heaven open, and the angels of God ascending and descending on the Son of Man."

In the dream of Genesis 28, Jesus is the Escala. Jesus is the ladder. Jesus is the stairway. When the cross fell into that hole, Jesus is the one who was crucified and opened heaven. He pierced heaven. From earth toward heaven, it was pierced because he had come down from heaven and was going to return to his Father. And because of what He did through Jesus, the offspring of Abraham, all nations would be blessed, and Jesus is the one who says, "...you shall see heaven open ...." Now what is characteristic of an open heaven? When heaven is open, there is activity between heaven's realm and earth's realm. When heaven is open, there are angelic beings ascending and descending. Jesus said to Philip, "I tell you the truth, you shall see heaven open, and the angels of God ascending and descending on the Son of Man." Now the Son of Man was not a humble title like Jesus saying little ole me. The Son of Man was the fulfillment of the prophesy in Daniel where it says, "I saw one coming from the Ancient of Days like unto the Son of Man." It was a Messianic title. He said:

"You shall see...the angels of God ascending and descending on me because I am the Son of Man of Daniel 9. I am the fulfillment, I am the Messiah and I am the Son of God. I am God become flesh and you are going to see angels ascending and descending on me."

Now, in the Bible I told you the two times that referenced when angels came and visited Jesus. But, this passage says to Nathanael that he is going to see angels ascending and descending on Jesus. Now we are not told in the Bible when that happened but I believe Nathanael saw it because Jesus is God and the Bible says that God is not a man that He should lie. So, we know from that inference that Jesus had these visitations more than the two times that we are told about in scripture because of what he said to Nathanael. We need to realize that Jesus is what this is all about. The open heaven happens because of Him. Here is the connection we need to make. We are the body of Christ on the earth today. Where is this open heaven supposed to be? Over us. We should have an understanding that under this open heaven there is angelic activity going on whether we can see it or not. We can understand that this was literally occurring upon the body of Christ, both in the historic context of Jesus and it is continuing to happen now in the life of His Body, the church. In other words, we are not left here alone. He said, "I will not leave you here alone." He meant He was going to send the Holy Spirit to us. But, I think we have limited so much of the New Covenant to our understanding of the contrast and difference of the role the Holy Spirit had between the Old Testament and the New Testament time. I want you to know that under the New Convenant there is a greater dimension and outpouring of the Holy Spirit unlike any the Old Testament people ever had. It is the same way when we compare the involvement of the angelic hosts between the New Covenant people and the Old Covenant people. One of the benefits of the cross of Jesus Christ is this open heaven with the Holy Spirit poured out and angelic activity. Both were a new dimension that came upon us, by grace, because of what Jesus accomplished at the cross.

Confirmation Through Experience

Now turn with me to Hebrews 1:14.

> Are not all angels ministering spirits sent to serve those who will inherit salvation.

There are a couple of things I want to explain further. The root of the word "ministering" is "diakonos", which is where we get the word deacon, which means someone who comes along and waits upon you and helps you. Therefore, not only is the Holy Spirit the great helper, but all angels are ministering spirits sent from heaven to earth and then back to heaven after serving those of us who will inherit eternal life. God created the angels to carry out his bidding, to worship him and to serve us. In verse 7, in speaking of the angels, he says:

> He makes his angels winds,
> his servants flames of fire.

I use to think that was poetry, I really did. I thought, "Isn't that pretty. It is even in a poetic form; it was meant to be poetry."

I believed that until I was in Volta Redonda, Brazil preaching to 3,000 people in a tent in a place where there weren't any windows. I said, (speaking metaphorically, poetically) "God send your wind through this place." They told me later that when I said that, the wind blew through and it really encouraged us. Wow! They said, "You said, "send your wind" and God did." Wasn't that a nice coincidence? At least that's what I thought.

We then went from there to Goiania, Brazil. In Goiania, I was on my knees worshipping during worship time when suddenly I felt this really strong wind hit me all at once. I opened my eyes. I thought somebody had twirled by me, maybe one of the women dancing had twirled around and caught the wind, but nobody was there. Nearby, there was a man from Atlanta, Georgia, named Mike. I then said, "Mike did you do that?" He said, "What?" I said, "Forget it." It was really getting weird. I thought I was getting weird; that I had been in Brazil too long. But then I thought, "God, what was that?" I then had this strong impression that God had sent his angels. I said: "Lord, how can I know that's not my head talking to me but really You? I mean if that was really You, I would like to know it; how can I know?" I got another impression to tell the people that God said angels are here and they are going to feel wind come across their face or pressure come on their shoulders or head and when they do, have them stand up and I will heal them without a word. Nobody will have to pray, it's just going to happen by them standing up because I am going to prove to you that angels are here. I thought, "That was weird. Was that God or just me?" Then, I thought, "I have to go for it because if I don't go for it, I will never know." But, it had been a really good meeting up to that point and worship had been great.

The previous night was wonderful. Faith was very high. I thought, "If I say that and it doesn't happen, it is going to kill this meeting; so wisdom says wait and do it at the very end. That way if you are wrong, it is not going to create too much damage." Then, I immediately had another thought, "No, do it now!" I knew that last one was not my thought because I had already had my good idea. Now listen, when you are not sure it's God you don't have to pretend you do. So, I said, "I think God just told me there are angels here and I think He said He was going to prove it to me because you are going to feel wind hit you or pressure come on your shoulders and if you will stand up, He will heal you without anybody saying a word. Nobody will pray for you. We are not going to do anything; we are just going to wait and He is going to do it. So if it happens, it was God and if it doesn't, it was me." You may say: "That sure doesn't build much faith." You know what, if it's really God you don't have to pretend your faith is higher than what it is. If it is really the Lord, just say what you think He said and let Him prove it. So I said: "I want everybody to be still and do not move or talk or create a false wind or anything. We are just going to wait five minutes starting now." Two of the longest minutes of my life went by without anything happening. In the third minute, people began to stand all over the place. At the end of it, I said: "Five minutes is up. Check your body out. How many of you were healed?" I then said: "If you were healed come down and tell us what you were healed of." Seventy-five people came down and told us of glorious healings. Nobody had said a word. God proved it to me. I was really getting excited.

God Reinforces His Point

Then, I was in Brazil another time in Volta Redonda, the

same place where the wind came through. This time my friend, Gary Oates, was taken out of his body into heaven and ultimately saw the Lord. (I won't relate his full story here. You can read it in its entirety in his book, Open My Eyes, Lord). When he came back into his body (I saw him come out of the trance into his body again), he was shot backwards and knocked down three rows of chairs and almost knocked a man down in the fourth row. There he was, this non-mystical type guy lying there weeping. Gary is an organizer and likes to stay in control, but God just apprehended him. Following that time, he began seeing angels. To this very day, he has this gift that comes every once in a while and he can see what is happening. Now you may say, this is all so subjective; what would make you really believe that what he experienced was real. Well, first of all, it totally freaked him out. He told me: "Randy, I think I may be going crazy. I need somebody to talk to." We were in a meeting in a big church of about 3,000 people and all of a sudden during a drama they were doing while the drums were being played, he saw a bunch of angels come out over the top of the crowd and he said: "They just went above us. I need somebody to talk to." Well, the worship leader was born with Down's syndrome and had been healed at six years old and taken to heaven eight times and could also see in the spirit realm. Afterwards, my friend went up to the worship leader and said: "Davi, when those drums were going did you see anything happen?" Davi said: "Yes, a bunch of angels came out from behind and went over the crowd." My friend looked at me and said: "I'm not crazy; I'm not losing my mind, I am beginning to see."

One night we had gone to Manaus, meeting in a church of about 21,000 at that time but which now has about 60,000 members. The first time we were there they didn't have any walls because they were building as money was received; they only had pillars, ceiling and concrete. This time when I was ministering for healing and said (I had just heard it thunder): "Oh God, let your river flow and let that river flow through here like in Ezekiel and Revelation and wherever the river touches, heal people." I no more than got that out of my mouth when it started pouring down rain. It began pouring down rain and then came the wind. I wasn't making connections yet; I still hadn't connected the dots in my mind and the wind blew the rain in the section over on the left side. Do you know who was seated there? That was the deaf section and they were getting sopped with water. In a matter of just a few minutes, we had eight deaf people who began hearing. We had our cameras and were asking which testimony should we get? It was glorious! In one of the videos, you can see that I caught the wind accidentally. The wind also went completely over this 10,000 seat sanctuary, the ceiling is thirty or forty feet high and you could see the wind swirl all the way across to the other side. People were getting healed all over the place. Now that hadn't happened when we were previously there. Can you imagine a church that seats 10,000? The wind blew the rain and the mist came in and touched our face up on the platform. The pastor said: "This has not happened since you guys were here before." As a matter of fact our team got a nickname. You know what our team is called in Manaus, Brazil? We found out on another trip there.. They nicknamed the team: "Wonder Workers". I like that name! My friend Gary Oates, the man whose eyes had been opened, was teaching. He had never fallen down while teaching. As he was teaching, I saw his eyes roll up and he fell down. I thought: "He's in trouble. He's on the floor and his mike is still on." I knew God was up to something. Gary's wife had also gotten drunk in the Spirit and her eyes were opened too. Anyway I said: "Kathy, go get the mike and take over." Kathy got up there and she is very prophetic. What happened was, Gary saw a 15 foot angel come right down the middle aisle and it just undid him. Kathy got up and did the most bizarre thing. Kathy grabbed the mike and started prophesying to the wind. I mean she literally prophesied to the wind and the wind started blowing inside the sanctuary—the walls were no longer open to the outside because construction had been completed. It blew so hard that it blew the back three rows of chairs over, it came up and we had a huge prop of a door on the platform about 2 inches thick and that door was blown open and the wind was not blowing outside the church. Earlier in that series of meetings, we had been doing what we do every night— asking that if people are 80% healed, wave two hands above your head, and we were seeing 500 to 800 a night get healed. That was only about 10% of the crowd of 5,000 to 8,000 a night. The last night we had over 10,000 people and Gary came up because I had been encouraging him to tell me what he was seeing. He said: "Randy, there are some warrior angels in this place tonight." I said: "How do you know they are warrior angels; how do you know these different kinds of angels?" He said: "I know they are warrior angels because they all have swords and are dressed like gladiators." I said: "Where are they?" He said: "They are over there in the balcony on that beam." I said: "What are they doing?" He said: "They are standing there like guards." I said: "Okay, keep me posted." So, we were ministering and a little bit later Gary came to me and said: "The warrior angels are on the move." I said: "What are they doing." He said: "They are clearing out the heaven. There are black blotches like demonic stuff and they are literally running away. They have the enemy on the run. Heaven is getting cleared out tonight. Heaven is getting opened tonight." I know some of you reading this must be saying: "This teaching is very weird. He is really off and this is getting kind of far out." You might be asking, "How do you know that was really God?" Well, I think I would have questions if I were you and only hearing somebody's subjective story. I would think this could all be a matter of imagination except for the fruit. That night it wasn't 500 or 800 people that got healed. That night, 9,000 of the 10,000 were waving their hands that they had received a healing in their body. The difference between that night and the other nights was the visitation of the warrior angels that cleared the heavens and gave us the open heaven in a greater way. To me, that is evidence that something was taking place.

By the way, one night I felt like the Lord was telling me to teach a sermon I had never taught before. I said, "What?" He gave me a scripture and I asked Him to give me more. But, that's all I got. I said, "God there are 10,000 people out there and you want me to teach something that I don't know what I'm going to say and all I have is a Scripture? There was only silence. I was warring mentally between going with this sermon I knew versus this text and not having any idea what I was going to say. The pastor was introducing me and I still didn't know which way I was going. Right in the middle of that when I was wondering what I should do, I started forward and then turned around to see who pushed me, but nobody was there. Actually, there was somebody there whom I couldn't see. So, I went with the text. That was all the encouragement I needed. I have many more stories which could reinforce this point.

Revelation of Wind and Fire

Let's quote Hebrews 1:7. Speaking of the angels, it says:

> "He makes his angels winds, his servants flames
> of fire." That's a quote from Psalm 103: 20 and
> 21 and 104: 3 and 4. Say it to yourself again:
> "He makes his angels winds, his servants flames
> of fire."

Turn to Acts 2:

> 1When the day of Pentecost came, they were all
> together in one place. 2Suddenly a sound like the
> blowing of a violent wind came from heaven and
> filled the whole house where they were sitting.
> 3They saw what seemed to be tongues of fire
> that separated and came to rest on each of them.
> 4All of them were filled with the Holy Spirit and
> began to speak in other tongues as the Spirit of
> God gave them utterance.

The wind and the fire were more than metaphors or signs of
the Holy Spirit. The sign of the Holy Spirit was the languages
given. If we really see the Scripture through Hebrews 1 and
Psalm 103, we understand that on the day of the outpouring
of the Spirit this was not simply a new relationship given by
grace to the Holy Spirit. There also was a new relationship
given by grace to the hosts of heavens, the angels, happening
at the same time. In Luke 3: 16 (there was a time when
I thought this was one of my weakest points until a Greek
scholar told me it's one of my best points.) it says:

> John the Baptist answered them all: "I baptize
> you with water, but one more powerful than I

will come, the thongs of whose sandals I am not worthy to untie. He will baptize you with the Holy Spirit and with fire."

Right? Note that it's not "as fire". What about "like fire?" No! It's what? It reads, "and fire." You know, this is interesting. "And" is a word for something in addition to. "As" and "like" are words of similitude. Such as, "it looked like this." In Greek it is "kai" which is like our "and". Jesus is going to baptize you with the Holy Spirit and He is going to baptize you with fire. We know that in one verse, it says: "He makes his servants flames of fire." Then one of the Baptist scholars wrote me and said, "But in the context there he is only talking about purification." And in another letter by email, this Greek scholar said: "I think you are pushing it too far." Then I realized that in one of the greatest stories in the whole Bible about consecration and call to the mission, we read in Isaiah 6: "Who shall go for me and whom shall I send?" I said, "Here am I, send me." That response follows after he said: "I am a man of unclean lips living among a people of unclean lips." God spoke to an angel and said, "Go over to the altar and pick up a coal of fire and bring it and touch his unclean lips." I then realized that scripture teaches that some of the activity of angelic beings is to bring a consecrating affect. The Holy Spirit and the angels do a lot of work in tandem. As a matter of fact in the Bible, God is often seen coming riding upon a white horse and the angels are his entourage.

In Exodus 3:2 (one of the most important events in the whole Bible as far as Old Testament History): There the angel of the Lord appeared to him in flames of fire from within a bush. Moses saw that though the bush was on fire it did not burn up.

In 2 Kings 2:11: As they were walking along and talking together, suddenly a chariot of fire and horses of fire appeared and separated the two of them, and Elijah went up to heaven in a whirlwind.

My friends, this is not Dorothy and Toto and a tornado in Kansas. These are angelic hosts that came to usher this great man of God into the presence of God. That's why in Psalm 103, looking back over the Hebrew history, the psalmist understood by the revelation of the Holy Spirit that this fire and this wind were angelic activities sent from God. That's what happened when, in the First Baptist Church at Advance, Missouri, the Holy Spirit fell after some had attended a conference in Southern Illinois. They were singing the Spirit Song by John Wimber in this First Baptist Church when all of a sudden they heard the sound of a mighty rushing wind in the church and everybody in the choir was slain in the Spirit. The pastor said: "I was so afraid that I got down and stuck my head under the chair and was afraid to look at what was going on. I heard shrieks, weeping and laughter. In the next few weeks, we saw almost every miracle recorded in the New Testament take place in our church."

As I look at my Bible, I can say, this is not a history book; this is the menu from which you can order. But if you don't know this book, you don't know what's right and what's not right to order. This Word of God is your menu of the wonderful things the Father has prepared for you because of the dream that was fulfilled in Jesus that opened heaven. As a matter of fact, the most common word for God in the Bible is Lord of Hosts, which tragically in the NIV is never translated that way. It is translated the Lord God Almighty because the translators felt that Lord of Hosts didn't make sense. Properly understand, He is the Lord over a host of angels fully prepared to do His bidding.

Fellow Servants

The last thing we will consider is Revelation 19:10 where John sees an angel, falls down at the angel's feet, and the angel of the Lord says: "Do not do it! I am a fellow servant with you and with your brothers who hold to the testimony of Jesus. Worship God!" First of all, the angel says, I am a fellow servant with you and with your brothers who hold to the testimony of Jesus. Secondly, what I want to emphasize here is that we never want to worship angels. We do need to let the pendulum swing back to a place of balance. The secular culture really believes in the angelic. It is inside the church that we think they are mythological and legendary and don't have a whole lot of faith in them. Or we feel they are historical way back then but God doesn't do it that way today. I am just trying to say, "Oh, what a great plan of salvation that He would love us so much." Don't worship the angels. May they not be the focus, but may you be aware that you are not alone. There is an air force and we have learned from the earthly wars that whoever controls the air, mops up on the ground. I am so glad our heavenly air force has their air force outnumbered 2 to 1 because only a third was cast out. There are at least two-thirds that remain faithful to the Lord who are fellow servants. I don't know if this makes the spiritual world more real, promises more real and scripture more relevant to today. So, I go back to the question that Omar Cabrera asked me, "Why don't we North Americans ask God to send his angels, as well as the Holy Spirit into our meetings?" I didn't tell you this next part because he also said, "The more angels you have in the meeting, the stronger the anointing in the meeting." Did you ever wonder why it says the angels are ascending and descending? If they have been here working, they are like us. They receive anointing. It's not their own; it is from God. We are wired 110 and that's why when we get too close to God, we short out. Angels, I believe, are wired 440. That's why they can enter into the throne room and that is also why we must have and will need glorified bodies. Anyway, I thank God for such a wonderful plan of salvation. I thank Him for the death of Jesus that made it possible and that's my focus and it is He whom we worship. And I am especially grateful that in Christ we can gain a fuller understanding of God's ways through these powerful open heaven experiences.

RANDY CLARK

{ Are You Thirsty? }

RANDY CLARK

I want to discuss an important doctrine that much of the Church believes was only for the early church, that we don't need any more because we have the Bible. However, 1 Corinthians 13 makes clear that the imperfect will not pass away until "the perfect is come." That's when prophecy shall cease and tongues shall pass away. Those who take the cessationist view believe those things have already ended and along with them the doctrine I want to share with you—impartation.

The cessationist view is that the sign gifts ended with the death of the Apostles, the disciples of the Apostles or the canonization of Scripture. Yet, we need to interpret Scripture as it would have been received by the initial recipients. In this case, the Church, the people Paul was writing to. And this is where F. F. Bruce and other famous New Testament scholars have said, "that which is perfect" does not refer to the Bible, but to Jesus Christ and His second coming.

During the Reformation, the focus was not on the gifts of the Holy Spirit, but on the role of the Holy Spirit in salvation, in bringing us to Christ and sustaining us in our relationship to Christ. The big issue of that time was "How are you really saved?"

Theology of the Kingdom

More recently, we've been hearing about the "Theology of the Kingdom." This is a teaching popularized by Fuller Theological Seminary Professor George Allen Ladd. A Baptist, Ladd saw that John the Baptist, Jesus, Paul, Peter and Phillip in Samaria preached the good news of the Kingdom of God. If you study Jesus' parables, you will find that the Kingdom of God doesn't get started and then stop, but it is ever-increasing, like the leaven in the dough that leavens the whole lump. Advancing the kingdom is one of the roles of the Holy Spirit.

The Gospel of the Kingdom is not just a Gospel of forgiveness of sin, it is a Gospel of the in-break of the Kingdom. With the coming of the Kingdom, power and authority has been given to the Church to bring the message of salvation, forgiveness, deliverance and healing. The Holy Spirit provides power for all of these—not just for forgiveness and regeneration, but also for casting out demons and bringing healing.

When you only focus on salvation, you have only a third of the Gospel, or maybe even less than that. God is concerned about more than just the Church, although it is the primary means through which God establishes His Kingdom on earth.

Impartation

So, what does impartation have to do with the coming of the Kingdom? I believe impartation is an important way that God touches us to bless us through the Holy Spirit and angels who carry out God's directions. I believe impartation is the most important call that God has placed on my life.

When I was pastoring 150 people in a village of 120 people, I went to see James Robison in 1984, at the James Robison

Bible Conference. Among the speakers at that conference was a man named John Wimber. When it came time to receive prayer, I felt unworthy of receiving anything, so I said to Wimber, "I am not worthy for you to pray for me, but I have some deacons with me. Will you pray for them?" And he grabbed my hand, and he said, "No, I am going to pray for you," and he prophesied many good things. I wish I had written them down, but I didn't have a tape recorder.

I didn't even know what prophecy was at the time. Coming from the Baptist tradition, we didn't have a whole lot of it. I later learned that the most famous Baptist teacher and preacher of all time—Charles H. Spurgeon from England—flowed in the gift of the word of knowledge. Not that he would have called it that.

Gifting Among Those Who Don't Believe in the Gifts

This is the wonderful thing about the Baptists—they make the gifts simpler. They just say, "The Lord told me." When I told my grandmother about the gifts, particularly the word of knowledge, she said, "Well, I have had that." I said, "You have?" She said, "Yeah!" And when I started talking about seeing people falling all over the place, she said, "Ohhhh! My goodness! Down at Lick Creek Baptist Church, there was a time that God came, and there were bodies everywhere. You had to step over them going out of the meeting."

I said, "Grandma, I didn't ever know about that." "Yeah, yeah, yeah! It happens all the time." You know, in that visitation it *was* happening all the time. She even told me about hearing the audible voice of God—one of the few people I've ever met who has.

She asked if I remembered Forrest Hunter—and I did. In a small church with 30 to 50 members, everyone knows who isn't saved—and everyone is praying for those people. When the Holy Spirit would come on one of those folks, you would see them tear up and look guilty. You would see them grab the pew in front of them until their knuckles turned white, till they finally got to a point that they resisted so much that they would harden their hearts.

So Forrest Hunter was one of those guys with a really hardened heart, and nothing seemed to touch him. My grandmother said, "Well, one night I was in the choir, and we were singing, and I heard God say, 'Tell Forrest that if he doesn't get saved tonight, he is going to die, and he will never be saved. This is the last chance for him.'" So I said, "Grandma! What did you do?" She said, "Well, what else can you do? I had to tell him. So after the choir was finished, I came up to him, and I said, 'Forrest, Jesus said that if you don't get saved tonight, you are never going to get saved, and you are going to die unsaved and go to hell.'"

I said, "Well, what did Forrest do? Did he get up and walk out the back of the church? Was he mad at you? What did he do?" She said, "No! He started crying, Randy, and he got saved."

Well, I want to tell you if someone takes that approach as their strategy for evangelism, all it is going to do is make people angry at them. However, if you have actually heard God tell you to tell somebody that this is their last chance, He will back it up. And in a moment, a guy who has been going to church for 40 years but never gotten saved, got saved—in that one moment, with that one prophetic word.

Now, my grandmother would not have called that a word of knowledge. She would just say, "The Lord told me."

Have you noticed that our hymnology is much better than our theology? For instance, "I come to the garden alone while the dew is still on the roses. And the voice I hear falling on my ear the Son of God discloses. And He walks with me and He talks with me and He tells me I am His own."

How can you say that God doesn't speak today and still sing that song? You see, our hymnology was better than our theology. Many Christians will agree that God speaks today as long as you don't try to categorize how He speaks as "prophecy," "words of knowledge" or something involving gifts of the Holy Spirit.

Life-Changing Prophecy

When I met John Wimber and he prophesied over me, I was very encouraged. I wanted to go to the city and plant a church, but I never had, and at that point I thought I never would. And John looked at me, and he said, "You are a prince in the Kingdom of God." That's a part I've never forgotten. After that, it wasn't very long before God came and touched my Baptist church. And it wasn't very long after that before I was out of the Baptist denomination, ending up in the Vineyard from 1984 until 2001.

Around 1984 or so, John asked me to be on the Council of the Vineyard movement. After I'd been on the council for a couple of years, I started feeling out of place. I really didn't have much to offer. I was talking to Blaine Cook, and I said, "These guys have more staff than I have people. I don't need to be on this thing anymore."

So I stepped off, because I was embarrassed that everybody on the council had 500 to 5,000 people in their churches. I didn't even have 50 yet. Vineyard people were teaching us how to break the 200 barrier, how to break the 400 barrier, how to break the 1,000 barrier, and I just wanted to break the 50 barrier! I was really embarrassed about being on the council. I was the oddball because I was the only guy who didn't have a big church. I realized later that the problem was my pride. I was just so humiliated being so little around these big guys.

I told Blaine all this, and Blaine said, "Didn't John tell you? Randy, you aren't on this council because of what you have. You are on this council because of what God is going to do with you. When John met you the first time at that James Robison Bible Conference, he heard the audible voice of God. He told me he did, and he has heard it twice about you."

And I said, "No! He never told me that!" Blaine said, "Don't you tell him I told you." And I never did. I just pretended that I was hearing it for the first time when John finally told me a few months before he died.

Actually, Blaine told me that God told John Wimber about two guys who would go all over the world and lay their hands on pastors and leaders to impart gifts and stir up things in them, in the baptism of the Spirit and the gifts. Blaine said, "You are one of those two." As a matter of fact, he said God told John that there is an apostolic call on my life.

But John didn't believe in apostles. Okay, so I have an apostolic call on my life, but John doesn't believe in apostles. I have got an apostolic ministry, but I'm not supposed to use the title. Okay. That's all right.

Tough Years Follow

I received John Wimber's prophecy in 1984, and the ten years that followed were ten of the hardest years of my life. I remember when I started a church in Saint Louis. I was really a great church planter. My wife and I went there, and we didn't know a soul. We would tell people, "Worship is our number one priority." But we didn't have a worship leader.

People would ask, "Do you have anything for the children?" No.

"Do you have any youth ministry?" No.

"Well, where do we go?" We don't have a building even; we just meet in the basement.

"Well, what do you have?" A vision of what it is going to be.

Well, it turned out that the only people interested in a church like that were people who didn't have any kids yet. After 11 months, we had the first 11 people. About two and a half to three years later, we had finally broken 50.

So, don't be discouraged. Just having a few people didn't mean that I didn't love God, and it didn't mean that I wasn't anointed. It just meant planting a church was a big task. Eight years later, when Toronto happened, we had about 400 in the church.

So when Toronto happened in 1994, John Wimber called me and said, "Randy, this is what God told me about you ten years ago (to the month!). Ten years ago I heard His audible voice, and you are now stepping into your destiny."

One of the most important things about Toronto was that the anointing God gave there was impartable; it was transferrable. In Brazil, there is no word "impartation" in Portuguese or if there is, it is not a common word, so we use the word "transference" to speak of imparting an anointing to someone else.

Before John Wimber died, I met with him, and we came to an Acts 15 agreement—I would go to the Pentecostals and the Charismatics, and he would continue the Vineyard's message to the Evangelicals. As it turned out, I have occasionally preached to the Baptists as well—the biggest Baptist churches in South Africa, Argentina and Brazil. However, at the time, in 1994, I had not received even one invitation outside of the Vineyard movement.

More Prophetic Words

Soon after that, however, Marc Dupont, who is a prophet, gave me another word. He said, "God is going to change your ministry really soon. God is going to start sending you to the Pentecostals, the Assemblies and even the Word of Faith. And I know your testimony, and I know that this one is going to really bother you."

And I said to him, "Listen! I don't know any Pentecostals. I don't have Pentecostal theology. I don't have any inroads in the Pentecostal movement, and if it happens, it will have to be God. And besides, I want to be in the Vineyard because I want to do what John is doing and reach the Evangelicals. That is my background."

"Well," he said, "that is going to change."

Now after that word, I went from 100% Vineyard invitations to 10%. And the other 90% of my invitations were suddenly Assemblies, Pentecostals and the Word of Faith. As a matter of fact, the first place that I went was a Word of Faith church, and God came. It was weird, but He came at this motorcycle club, with these huge guys with beards and black leather. We thought it would be really good for them to be the ushers to take up the offering.

Word of Faith churches only believe in two offices—pastors and teachers—not evangelists, prophets or apostles, so I didn't expect much from the offering. But I was surprised—it was three times the usual amount I received, with the same number of attendees. The point is, God was in control.

A Word of Caution

At the same time, I want you to understand that we will face challenges. You can have a great impartation, and you can be highly anointed, but you need to know that the greater the anointing, the stronger the counterattack from the enemy to try and bring you down.

I told you that John Wimber said two had received the apostolic anointing. What I didn't say was that the other person fell. At the time he fell, he was preparing to go to Brazil, and I wound up going there instead. For all that God has done in Brazil through me, I was actually His second choice. And I do believe in restoration, and I've invited this man to come with me and share any platform in the world, but he hasn't accepted that invitation yet.

As Christians we should be praying for each other, because people in the occult purposely target pastors and leaders.

And the more that God is using you, the more the occult people will pray against you. Those attacks don't excuse our falling, failure or sin. But we need to be aware of them and pray for each other. If we fall, we must confess our sins, don't beat ourselves up and seek restoration as David did after he sinned with Bathsheba and had Uriah killed.

There are others that God has greatly used who have fallen as well, including some recently. Now, we can point our fingers and begin to accuse, or we could lift our voices in prayer, asking God to bring restoration to this man and to his family. The fact that there is a problem now does not mean that everything that happened in this man's ministry wasn't God. It just means that there has been an attack and a deception that has come against one of God's chosen ones and that a chosen vessel, a sovereign choice, is now in trouble.

Anointing for Today

We need to be aware of what God is doing today, as well as what He did in the past that's recorded in the Scriptures. I want you to understand that He didn't quit. He didn't get tired. He didn't run out of power. He didn't run out of gifts.

Even some of the most famous Evangelicals understand that. Case in point: Calvinists do not believe that the gifts continued after the canonization of the Scripture, but Calvin taught that if you were going into a new area, a country or a region where there was an unreached people group who had never heard the Gospel, where there was no Church established, you could expect and should expect that the gifts would be restored to the Church until it gets established, and then they would die out again. At least he believed it was possible. I didn't know that until a couple years ago, and I got real excited and said, "Oh yeah, Calvin! All right."

Now, let's look at the Scripture. In Matthew 11:12, Jesus said, "From the days of John the Baptist until now, the kingdom of heaven has been forcefully advancing, and forceful men lay hold of it." Or as the King James version says, "...the kingdom of heaven suffereth violence, and the violent take it by force."

Are you so desperate and so hungry in your heart that you are not going to be passive? Are you going to be one of those violent ones who want to lay hold of the kingdom and not let go? Many people don't have that kind of hunger; they didn't get saved that way.

When those people are asked, "Well, what do you want?" they say, "Well, I don't know—whatever God wants to give me." Sometimes I am walking down the line, praying for people, and I ask what they want. They say, "Oh! I want the gift of healing. I want miracles. I want prophecy. That's what I want. I want the gift of tongues. I want to be able to interpret tongues. I want the gift of evangelism with power."

And then I get some people who say, "Oh, I don't know, just whatever He wants to give me." I don't have much faith for that one, because I know there isn't really any hunger there. There is not really any thirst there. That person is basically a passive Christian.

In the average church, 20 percent of the people give 80 percent of the money and do 80 percent of the work. That's true whether it is a Baptist church or a Roman Catholic church. The numbers are the same. Essentially, you have the dedicated carrying the freeloaders. The passive people are just not hungry for anything.

Hungry for God

But there is another group in the church, and they are passionate. God gives us that hunger. He is the one who draws us. If you will respond to Him, your passion will grow, or you can ignore it, and it will die.

Maybe you are one of those people who have been crying out, hungry, not satisfied, wanting more. You have heard the stories of what God is doing all over the world, and every time you hear the stories you say, "Oh! I didn't know that God was doing that. I want to do it, too!"

That is why I love to get around people who believe more than I do, see more than I do. When they tell me something that I didn't know was possible until I hear their stories, then I can say "God, I want that! I would like to do that, too."

Are you like that? Do you hear the stories and say, "Ah, I want to do it, too!"

Paul talked about it in Romans 9-11, about the Jewish people seeing what was going to happen amongst the Gentile church. What God did among the Gentiles would make the Jews jealous. Paul said the sign of His presence on us would make them jealous, so that at the end time, the nation will be restored into the one Body.

Just as Paul wanted to provoke the Jews to jealousy, I want you to hear about what God is doing and get jealous. I hope you will get hungry; you will get thirsty, and your faith will begin to rise.

A Failed Beginning

It's important for you to know that I actually began my ministry as a failure. John Wimber told me I was a prince. But, before that, I was kicked out of seminary. I was told that I could never have a ministry, and I was put on the dump heap. This is all true, the good, the bad, and the ugly. It's in my book *Lighting Fires*.

I was put on the dump heap, but God is the Great Reclaimer. He went to the dump heap and found somebody who was told "You will never have a ministry. Don't even waste our Southern Baptist money or your time. Go to law school. This is for your own good. You are over; it is over."

Well, I got depressed and flunked the test. Actually, I got angry, because there was a lot of rejection there. I didn't do very well there for a while and fell into sin. I went out and drank—something I hadn't done even when I was backslidden because my grandfather was an alcoholic before he got saved and God delivered him. I smoked dope while I was backslidden, but I didn't drink.

What I want you to understand is that it's not about what other people say about you that determines your success. It's about God and His power. It's about how hungry you are and how desperately you want Him to use you and how willing you are to yield to Him so He can use you.

God Can Use Anyone

2 Chronicles 16:9 says, "For the eyes of the Lord range throughout the earth to strengthen those whose hearts are fully committed to him…" God is looking for the people through whom He can show Himself strong. You might say

that God can show Himself strong through anybody. Yes, He could, but He won't violate anyone's will. He is looking for someone who wants to be so totally surrendered and so yielded that they would love to be one of the chosen ones of God who get to do some of these things.

When I was 19 years old, 11 of us from my little Baptist church went to a Christian college. We used to say that we could all be Billy Graham, and, you know, I think God liked that faith, but I don't think that it is good theology. We all can't be Billy Graham. We all can't be Benny Hinn. God is sovereign, and He elects and He chooses. But at the same time, even if He chooses us, we have to say YES!

I hope and pray that in your heart as you are reading this you are saying, "Lord, if You will touch me, if You will anoint me, I will go anywhere. I will do anything if You will just anoint me." That is what I prayed when I heard about Rodney Howard-Browne, who went through about eight years in the desert. I said, "Lord, if You will touch me one more time through an impartation from Rodney, I want to be one of those thousand who he said would get the same anointing that is on him, to help him take the Revival all over the world." I didn't think that I would get to be one of those thousand, but I wanted to be.

I prayed, and I said, "Lord, if You would touch me, I will go anywhere and do anything." I thought that it would be an invitation 20 miles away or an invitation across town. I would be glad to get an invitation. I hadn't had one invitation to preach anywhere in about 14 years. It was one of those sudden things, but I had really gotten excited when I heard his testimony.

I had no idea that God was going to do exceedingly and abundantly above all I could ask or think. But He has. Since Rodney prayed for me, God has taken me to 36 nations, and I have had an invitation to almost every nation in the world. I was a "little ole' me," a discard, a failure. I was the one who had been kicked out of school.

Now, I did go back to school, and I did graduate, but I had to jump through a whole lot of hoops to get back in. But the point is, I have never forgotten what happened. I want you to know that I know I am nothing. I know I have failed Him.

I am like a Peter, and all the rest of my life I will always know where I have failed Him. I shared that in *Lighting Fires*, and pastors who've been ready to quit and have read that book have called me. They've said, "I wept and wept as I read your book. I thought that God had to be done with me, but when I read the book and learned what He did with you, I know there is hope for me."

Willing to Serve Wherever

That is why I want to be a person of grace. I know what man's judgment can do and how it can destroy. It was only the belief in God's call that got me through it. Not only had I been kicked out of school, my own denomination was trying to take my ordination away from me. In the middle of that I was hurt and bitter.

I was no longer the chosen one, the one being groomed to get one of the largest churches in the association. Now, I was a reject. I was a failure. And I felt all of that. I got so discouraged, and I got angry, and I said, "God, how could You let this happen to me?"

You see, my first wife had had several adulterous affairs, and we had gotten a divorce while I was in my first semester of seminary. Divorce was unacceptable at that seminary and in that association. So I said, "God, how could You let this happen to me? I burned every bridge. I burned it all. All I can do is preach the Gospel, and now, Lord, they tell me that I can't, that I will never have a church."

So, I had failed, and I was drinking. I came home one night, and I was tipsy, and I had a vision. Now, I have only had a few visions. In this one, my favorite pastor, Dr. Smith from my college, said to me, "Randy, if you go back to where you came from, you are going to have a lot of rejection in your life. I just want to ask you a question." And Dr. Smith said, "Do you love the Church of Jesus enough to serve her when she hurts you?" And I said yes.

"Yes," I said, and I started crying. "Lord, they tell me I will never have a ministry. They tell me it is over. But I believe that You are the all-knowing one, and that You know everything from the beginning. You knew what was going to happen in my life, and yet You called me. And though man has rejected me, I think You have accepted me, so I am going to put my faith in Your call rather than in their judgment."

And I want you to understand that the most important part of that prayer is what I said next. Since that time, God has blessed me and used me beyond anything I could have ever dreamed. But you need to know that I didn't know He would. I just knew that I was called, and wherever He wanted me to serve, I had to be there.

So, I said, "If it means, Lord, that the best I ever do in the ministry is working a second job because the church is so small, that all I ever have is this rural church and I have to pump gasoline on the side to make a living, if that is all You have for me, then let me be faithful to the day I die, serving You in that place. But if You have more, then God, I just thank You."

Beyond Our Failures

So, God is able to use us even after we fail. Our failures do not disqualify us from serving Him. I wanted you to know where I came from, where I started. Somebody once asked me, "How do you stay humble?" I said, "Well, it is easy if you have a healing ministry. You have enough failure to keep you humble." But I also remember where I've come from and what God has done.

You may have experienced a major failure in your life, and if you have, the enemy is more than ready to use it against you. When you come home to be rededicated, the enemy wants to ensure that you will not have enough faith to go into the place where the table is set and the Father is waiting for you. He doesn't want you to feel like you can sit at the main table in the House of God and be fully restored as a son or daughter.

Even today, most of us come back to God as though we are the Prodigal son, saying, "I am no longer worthy to be called Your son. Just make me like one of Your hired servants." We feel like we can no longer do some of the things that God was calling us to do. We say, "I can't sing on the worship team. I can't teach Sunday School. I can't be an elder. I can't be WHATEVER. But I can mow the yard and clean the windows. Just make me a servant, but no longer the son with a full inheritance."

I just want to tell you that Jesus' parable of the Prodigal son wasn't just about forgiveness—it was about total restoration. The problem is that we have so many elder brothers yelling judgments that it is hard to hear the Father's voice over theirs sometimes.

Six Foundational Teachings of Christianity

Hebrews 6:1-2 lists for us the six foundational teachings of Apostolic Christianity. These are the foundational, elementary teachings, the most important six doctrines of the New Testament. Yet the Church no longer perceives one of these as a doctrine any more. The writer of Hebrews says, "Therefore let us leave the elementary teachings about Christ and go on to maturity," and then he begins to list the foundations of the faith. They include:

1. Repentance from acts that lead to death
2. Faith in God
3. Laying on of hands
4. Baptisms (plural, not singular)
5. Resurrection of the dead
6. Final judgment.

Those are the doctrines, and I want to focus on the third and the fourth—laying on of hands and baptisms, which includes both water baptism and the baptism of the Holy Spirit.

Baptism of the Holy Spirit

Now, my personal belief, discussed in detail in my book *The Baptism of the Spirit* is that the Pentecostals are wrong to say that you have to speak in tongues to be baptized in the Holy Spirit. Now, I don't want to offend anybody, but that would mean that nobody could have been baptized in the Holy Spirit, even though they led whole nations to the Lord, worked signs and wonders and moved in great power throughout the history of the Church. I just can't believe that. But I can't believe what the Evangelicals say either — that you get everything at conversion. I know that I have gotten a whole lot more since I got saved.

In Acts 1:4-5, Jesus told His disciples to wait in Jerusalem "for the gift my Father promised, which you have heard me speak about. For John baptized with water, but in a few days you will be baptized with the Holy Spirit." Then in Acts 1:8, He said, "But you will receive power when the Holy Spirit comes on you; and you will be my witnesses in Jerusalem, and in all Judea and Samaria, and to the ends of the earth." Jesus makes the connection between the coming of the Holy Spirit in response to the Father's promise and empowerment.

I have heard Rodney Howard-Browne, who is a Pentecostal, say a lot of people think they have been baptized in the Holy Spirit because they spoke in tongues. Because they received a prayer language, they thought they received the baptism of the Holy Spirit. Yet now they are no longer pursuing the power of God, because they think that having a prayer language means they have been baptized by the Spirit. I think that the Pentecostals say that the initial evidence is speaking in tongues, but that can end up shifting the focus to receiving tongues, instead of focusing on receiving the power of God.

Pentecostals used to ask me, "Have you got the Baptism," or "Do you have the Spirit?" Don't ask Christians, "Do you have the Spirit?" because as Paul said in Romans 8, if you don't have the Spirit of Christ, you don't belong to Him. What they really mean is there is more. And I wrote a book called *There is More*. And there is more after you get baptized in the Holy Spirit. You can get baptized again or filled. You can be filled again, and you can be refilled.

Transferring the Anointing

The very first time we see this in Scripture is in Numbers 11:16. God spoke to Moses and told him to bring 70 of Israel's elders to the Tent of Meeting, and He would come down to speak with all of them. Then in Numbers 11:17, God says, "…I will take of the Spirit that is on you and put the Spirit on them. They will help you carry the burden of the people so that you will not have to carry it alone."

Now, this is not something that Moses did. I want you to understand this. This is not Moses. Moses simply obeyed God and gathered the elders and brought them to the Tent of Meeting. It was God's choice to take the anointing that was on Moses—his call and gifting to bring the people out of Egypt and be their judge. God said, "You need help, and so I am going to take that same anointing that is on you, and I am going to put it on them."

That is supernatural empowerment, and there was no laying on of hands there, but it is the first time in the Bible that you see the transference of the anointing. Deuteronomy 34:9 says, "Now Joshua son of Nun was filled with the spirit of wisdom because Moses had laid his hands on him…." In 1Timothy 4:14, Paul says, "Do not neglect your gift which was given you through a prophetic message when the body of elders laid their hands on you."

So Paul tells us that Timothy got a gift, probably during his ordination service. But then in 2 Timothy 1:6, he says to

Timothy, "For this reason I remind you to fan into flame the gift of God, which is in you through the laying on of my hands." In Acts 19:6, we are told that after Paul baptized the believers at Ephesus, he laid his hands upon them, and the Holy Spirit came upon them, and they spoke in tongues and prophesied.

In Acts 8:18-19, Simon the magician—not someone who did magic tricks but someone involved in the occult who moved in the power of the demonic and held people in his power—saw a greater power in the Gospel of the Kingdom. Peter and John were visiting Samaria, and a lot of people had been healed. There was great joy in the city, and Simon also believed.

So, Simon the magician said to Peter, "I want to give you money so that whoever I lay my hands on will receive the Holy Spirit." And Peter said, "You and your money can go to hell." Simon then said, "Please pray that this doesn't happen to me." He thought that you could BUY the Holy Spirit.

Holy Spirit as a Deposit

Paul's writings tell us a lot about the Holy Spirit. Gordon D. Fee wrote a book called *God's Empowering Presence*, about 800 pages, in which he took every reference to the Holy Spirit in the writings of the Apostle Paul. Fee's conclusion was that the second most important doctrine from the Apostle Paul was this: "You are justified by faith."

Now, most of us would say that was Paul's most important doctrine, but no, Fee said that was his second most important. More important is how you can know if you have been justified. You know by the witness of the Spirit. That is your guarantee. That is the down payment, the deposit.

In Galatians 3:2, Paul writes, "I would like to learn just one thing from you: Did you receive the Spirit by observing the law, or by believing what you heard?" That question implies you had to be able to know that you had received the Spirit, because if you didn't know you had received the Spirit, that argument doesn't make sense. You had to know "I received the Spirit." It has to be self-authenticated.

When I visited Russia, our worship team began to play Christian music near a sports arena. One guy got so interested that he walked with us all the way back from the sports center, several miles to the hotel, bottle of vodka in hand. He was pretty tipsy, but he had lots of questions because he grew up Communist in atheist Russia, and he didn't know anything about the Christian faith, but he wanted to know more. I was trying to explain, and it was hard between his little bit of English and my very little bit of Russian to make the connection.

I asked God for a word of wisdom, and he gave me one, along with a translator who helped. I know some might have a problem with this illustration, but it made sense to him. I said, "Do you believe that the vodka in that bottle will make you drunk?"

He said, "Dah!"

And I looked at him and I said, "Do you really, really believe that the vodka in that bottle will make you drunk?"

"Oh, yeah! Dah! Dah! Dah!"

I asked him four or five times, and finally I said, "Do you believe that the vodka IN THE BOTTLE will make you drunk?"

Ahhhhh! It hits him. "No!"

I said, "Then how does the vodka make you drunk?"

"You have got to get it out of the bottle and into you," he said.

"That's the way you get saved," I said, "Does anybody have to tell you when you got the vodka out of the bottle and into you, or is it self-authenticating?"

He said, "Nobody has to tell me! I can feel the effects of it when it is in me."

I said, "In our country we call alcohol 'spirits,' but there is a Holy Spirit, and when He comes into you, just like that vodka, nobody is going to have to tell you. He just comes, and you know. Your faith that causes Him to come in then is self-authenticating, and you know you have genuine faith because of the witness of the effect of the Spirit that is in you." Then my Russian friend understood clearly.

Thirsty for More

When we receive the Holy Spirit, we know it. When we are thirsty, and want more of God and seek Him with all our hearts, He will give us more of Himself. There is more, and I hope you are thirsty and calling out to God for what you desire from Him. He wants you to ask, and He longs to respond. Don't let go of the hem of His garment until you have been filled and re-filled with the Holy Spirit, until you have received all that you ask for—and more.

OTHER BOOKS BY RANDY CLARK

Entertaining Angels

There Is More

Power, Holiness and Evangelism

Lighting Fires

God Can Use Little Ole Me

Essential Guide to Healing

Healing Unplugged

OTHER BOOKLETS BY RANDY CLARK

Evangelism Unleashed

Healing Ministry and Your Church

Learning to Minister Under the Anointing

TRAINING MANUALS AVAILABLE

Ministry Team Training Manual

Schools of Healing and Impartation Workbooks

CORE MESSAGE SERIES

Words of Knowledge

Biblical Basis of Healing

Baptism in the Holy Spirit

Open Heaven / Are You Thirsty Pressing In

The Thrill of Victory / The Agony of Defeat

Awed By His Grace / Out of the Bunkhouse

Healing is in the Atonement / Power of the Lord's Supper

Christ in You the Hope of Glory / Healing and the Glory

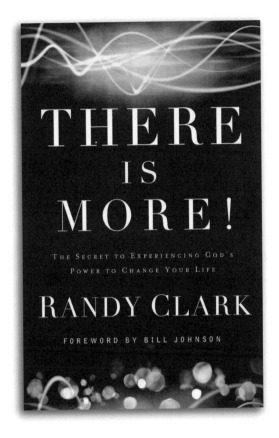

In *"There Is More"*, Randy lays a solid biblical foundation for a theology of impartation as well as taking a historical look at impartation and visitation of the Lord in the Church. This is combined with many personal testimonies of people who have received an impartation throughout the world and what the lasting fruit has been in their lives. You are taken on journey throughout the world to see for yourself the lasting fruit that is taking place in the harvest field - particularly in Mozambique. This release of power is not only about phenomena of the Holy Spirit, it is about its ultimate effect on evangelism and missions. Your heart will be stirred for more as you read this book.

"This is the book that Randy Clark was born to write."

- Bill Johnson

Global School of Supernatural Ministry

Vision

To release followers of Christ into their specific destiny and calling, in order to live out the Great Commission.

Structure

Global School of Supernatural Ministry is a one or two year ministry school with an emphasis on impartation and equipping students for a life of walking in the supernatural. Classes start each September and end the following May. Courses are offered on-site at the Apostolic Resource Center in Mechanicsburg, PA. Upon completion of each program year a Certificate of Completion is awarded. Students seeking additional educational training may do so while attending GSSM through the Wagner Leadership Institute.

Community

The GSSM student body is diverse in age, culture, ministry experience, and educational accomplishments. From high school graduates to professionals to retirees - the students come together seeking more of God. Supernatural power, passion and honor are key values of GSSM and are reflected in our worship, outreach and personal relationships.

For more information - or to enroll in classes - contact us at:
1-866-AWAKENING or apply online at:
http://gssm.globalawakening.com

globalawakening

For a schedule of upcoming events and conferences,
or to purchase other products from Global Awakening,
please visit our website at:

www.globalawakening.com